RISE UP

AND

ℬUILD

A Biblical Approach to Dealing
With Anxiety and Depression

DANA RONGIONE

RISE UP

AND

$\mathscr{B}$UILD

A Biblical Approach to Dealing With Anxiety and Depression

DANA RONGIONE

All Scripture notations are taken from The Holy Bible, KJV.

Copyright © 2017 Dana Rongione

Rise Up and Build

It was such a hot day—almost as hot as my temper. Too hot to walk home, especially with the news I had to share. I rehearsed the speech over and over again in my head during that strenuous trek, yet when I finally arrived at my house, I still didn't have the words to explain to my dad how my truck (with my mom and myself inside) had ended up lying on its side in the ditch. I wanted to blame my mom. She was the one who had been grabbing at the steering wheel while trying to teach me to drive. I, however, was the one who had thrown up my hands and declared, "Fine, if you want to drive, have at it!"

She tried, but from the passenger seat, there's only so much one can do to avoid the—ahem—pitfalls of driving. So we crashed. Into the ditch. The truck lying on its side with one wheel hovering two feet off the ground as it was held suspended over the ditch. There was no way we were driving the vehicle out. There was only one thing to do —go get Dad and a tow rope.

I will never forget that day. The day I allowed my emotions to get the best of me and endangered my life and the life of my mom. That experience will be forever etched in my brain as the day I gave up control. I took my hands off the wheel and left my life up to chance. I wish I could say I never made the same mistake again after that horrible incident, but that would be a lie. Yes, it would seem that I was destined for a life of giving up control and casting blame elsewhere for the disastrous results that ensued. It wasn't a steering wheel I was letting go of but rather my emotional and physical health —my spirit.

He that hath no rule over his own spirit is like a city that is broken down, and without walls. (Proverbs 25:28)

Broken down. Does that sound familiar? Broken. Downhearted. Confused. Afraid. Frustrated. Hopeless. If you can relate to any of these feelings, then I'm so glad you're reading this book. I understand how you feel because I've been there. I have sensed I was imprisoned by emotions I seemingly had no control over. I am all too familiar with the ups and downs of life's roller coaster. Happy one day. Discouraged beyond belief the next. It appeared I had no rule over my spirit, and just as the Bible says, I was broken down and defenseless against every dart the devil threw my way.

People tried to help me as I'm sure they've tried to help you. They offered sound advice like "You need to get over it" and "Don't think about it." And, of course, let's not forget the three little words that cause most of us to burst into song: "Let it go!" (Thanks, Elsa.) Obviously, these people have been gifted with a happiness switch we seem to lack. While they mean well, their words might as well be snowflakes falling into an open flame because, the truth is, we know what to do. We comprehend what the Bible says, and Heaven knows we've tried to put it into practice, but as one of my favorite movie lines states, "The concept is grasped; the execution is a little elusive." We know what to do, but we can't figure out how to do it. How do we control our thoughts and emotions? How can we let go of things that seem to be burned into our memories? Is there hope for the Humpty Dumpties of this world who seem broken beyond compare?

Let's ask Nehemiah, for he knows a thing or two about being broken down. In the book of Nehemiah, the prophet by the same name was burdened by the Lord to take on an impossible task—to rebuild the wall of Jerusalem. Understand, this wall wasn't just weak or wobbly, it had crumbled and was lying in heaps of rubble. Nevertheless, where others saw brokenness, Nehemiah saw an opportunity and set out to do the impossible. Not only did he and the people rebuild the wall, but they did it in a mere fifty-two days despite the many obstacles hurled their way. Nehemiah had a burden, and he could not escape God's plan for him. In that, I understand how he felt.

I am burdened for you, but I must tell you I'm not writing this book because I have overcome all depression and anxiety but rather because the Lord has revealed the way out of my prison, and while I haven't reached complete freedom, I know I am well on my way. The light is shining so much brighter than it ever has before, and for the first time, the victorious Christian life seems like more than a distant dream. But let me tell you this: this journey is not for the faint of heart. If you're looking for a quick fix or an easy three-step system to release the shackles of anxiety and depression, you might as well stop reading now. The method I will reveal in the following pages will take time, effort and a willingness on your part to give it your all (which we will talk more about in the next couple of chapters). I tell you this now because I want you to understand what you're getting yourself into.

The sad truth is that many of us are anxious and depressed because we've given up control of our emotions just as I gave up control of my truck all those years ago. It wasn't taken from us. We gave it up willingly whether we realize it or not. That being said, what is there left to do but cast blame for our current emotional state? We blame it on circumstances or heredity, and while those things factor in to anxiety and depression, they are not the reason we suffer. We suffer because we refuse to take responsibility for our own actions and reactions. We use phrases like "I can't help it" and "It's just the way I am" to excuse poor choices and point the finger at some other factor that must be the cause of all our pain. But when we shift the responsibility elsewhere, all we are doing is reinforcing our feelings and attitudes of being helpless and out of control. If we want to change our lives and banish the negativity, we need to get our hands back on the wheel and take control. In the pages to follow, I'll take you step-by-step through the process of owning your pain and taking responsibility for the emotions you allow into your life.

Using the key verse of Proverbs 25:28 and the story of Nehemiah, I hope to enlighten you on why we struggle with our emotions and how to protect ourselves from anxiety and depression. For starters, I want you to imagine that your heart is a city. Without the proper protection, it is vulnerable to attack from all sides, and once the heart is conquered, the battle is all but lost.

Proverbs 4:23 warns us, *Keep thy heart with all diligence; for out of it are the issues of life.* To keep means to protect, so how do we protect our hearts? By building walls around it. Now, I know that sounds odd since we're often told not to build walls around our hearts because it keeps people out. But these aren't walls to keep out friends and family. These are walls intended to keep out the enemy. They are walls of protection against Satan's fiery darts and evil intentions. Without such walls, just as Proverbs 25:28 tells us, our city will be broken down. If we want to keep depression and anxiety at bay, we must rise up and build the four walls that surround our hearts. Those walls are: (1) The Wall of the Mind, (2) The Wall of the Tongue, (3) The Wall of the Ears, and (4) The Wall of the Eyes. With the right foundation and sturdy walls, we will be able to protect our hearts. We don't have to be victims to our emotions or circumstances. We can be victors by building up our defenses against the enemy. So, if you're ready to be free from the chains of doubt, confusion, fear and discouragement, grab a hammer and a trowel, and let's rise up and build!

INSPECT YOUR FOUNDATION

HAVE YOU BUILT UPON THE ROCK?

In Nehemiah 2, the prophet rode out at night to inspect the damage to the city walls. While the Bible doesn't specifically state what he was looking for, I have no doubt that one thing he was checking on was whether there was still a solid foundation to build upon.

You don't have to be a carpenter, mason or architect to know you need a solid foundation before starting a building project. No matter how thick or tall the walls, if they are built on a weak foundation, it won't be long before they topple and fall. That being said, before we build up the walls around the heart, let's check our foundation.

The Bible makes it very clear that without Christ, we can do nothing. Nothing! If

15

you do not have a saving knowledge of Jesus Christ, you may as well quit now, for you'll never find the peace and joy for which you are searching outside of Him. He is joy! He is peace! And if you want freedom, you can only find it at His feet. I'm not talking about religion. I'm talking about a relationship with the King of Kings and Lord of Lords. If you don't know what that means, allow me to explain.

Long ago, God created the world, and in it, he placed a man named Adam and a woman named Eve. Despite having everything they could want or need, the couple disobeyed God and ate the forbidden fruit of the garden in which He had placed them. This act of disobedience brought sin into the world, and everyone that has existed since that time has been born with a sin nature. Whether you feel you're a "good person" or not doesn't matter. The fact is we are all sinners, meaning we are all guilty of some wrong, whether it be lying, stealing, being proud or whatever. We are all guilty!

But that created another problem because God wants us to dwell with Him in Heaven when the time comes for us to die

RISE UP AND BUILD

or for Him to take us home, but there is no sin in Heaven. It isn't allowed, which means, we aren't allowed. That is, not unless there was a way to cleanse us from our sin. Fortunately, there was, but that way cost God's Son, Jesus, His life. He died in our place and took our sins upon Himself in a gruesome display of love and compassion. And because of His sacrifice, everyone now has the opportunity to join God in Heaven. Notice I said everyone has the opportunity, not that everyone will go. Why? Because God has given each of us a choice. We can accept Jesus as Lord of our lives and be saved, or we can refuse His great gift, failing to acknowledge our need of a Savior. It's up to us, but I warn you there is a horrible fate awaiting those who refuse this offer.

If you don't know Jesus, and you would like to accept Him and His great sacrifice, God has made it as easy as A-B-C.

A — Admit you're a sinner and in need of a Savior. It's impossible to be saved from something if you won't acknowledge you need saving. Romans 3:23 tells us, *For all have sinned and come short of* *the glory of God. In other words, we can't get to Heaven on our own.*

B — Believe that Jesus Christ is the Son of God, who came willingly to die on the cross to pay the debt for our sins and then rose again to return to Heaven, awaiting the day God will call all His children home to live with Him for all eternity. Because of His sacrifice, we can have eternal life. *For God so loved the world, that he gave his only begotten Son, that whosoever believeth in him should not perish, but have everlasting life. (John 3:16)*

C — Confess that Jesus is Lord of your life. The Bible tells us that even the devils believe and tremble. Belief is a vital step, but you must put that faith into action by surrendering your life and your will into God' hands. Give Him control of everything you have and everything you are. *That if thou shalt confess with thy mouth the Lord Jesus, and shalt believe in thine heart that God hath raised him from the dead, thou shalt be saved. (Romans 10:9)*

If you've never heard the salvation message, I'm sure this sounds complicated and confusing, but I assure you it isn't meant to be. Still, if after reading this you feel you don't understand what it means to have a personal relationship with Christ, please contact me through my website, DanaRongione.com. I would love to talk with you and walk you through the process. Whatever you do, don't skip this step. This is the most important decision you'll ever make, and it will determine the rest of you life. Please, choose Jesus today!

WHAT IF I'M ALREADY SAVED?

I have heard it said real Christians do not get depressed or anxious. I say these people need to read their Bibles a little more carefully. It is evident that some of the "greats" in the Bible were anxious or depressed from time to time. Take David, for example. Or Elijah. Or Moses. Or Gideon. Each of these mighty men exemplified anxiety or depression at least once. So, Christian or not, depression and anxiety are real and can affect even the most devout lover of God.

Even Nehemiah became depressed when he found out about the destruction of the wall of Jerusalem. *And it came to pass, when I heard these words, that I sat down and wept, and mourned certain days, and fasted, and prayed before the God of heaven. (Nehemiah 1:4)* In fact, he was so distraught that four months later, the king whom he served asked what was wrong because he could tell by the prophet's countenance that he wasn't his usually cheerful self. *Wherefore the king said unto me, Why is thy countenance sad, seeing thou art not sick? this is nothing else but sorrow of heart. Then I was very sore afraid. (Nehemiah 2:2)*

Without a doubt, depression affects believers and nonbelievers alike, but the difference is that we, as Christians, don't have to fight the battle alone. We have someone with us.

That being said, it is always a good idea to examine our hearts and make sure we are right with God. Is there unconfessed sin in our lives? Are we habitually doing things we know are wrong and shrugging them off as no big deal? If we are serious about wanting to rid ourselves of anxiety and depression, we need to make sure we're starting off with a clean slate. God has promised if we will confess our sins, He will forgive us. Look at Nehemiah's example:

And said, I beseech thee, O Lord God of heaven, the great and terrible God, that keepeth covenant and mercy for them that love him and observe his commandments: Let thine ear now be attentive, and thine eyes open, that thou mayest hear the prayer of thy servant, which I pray before thee now, day and night, for the children of Israel thy servants, and confess the sins of the children of Israel, which we have sinned against thee: both I and my father's house have sinned. We have dealt very corruptly against thee, and have not kept the commandments, nor the statutes, nor the judgments, which thou commandedst thy servant Moses. Remember, I beseech thee, the word that thou commandedst thy servant Moses, saying, If ye transgress, I will scatter you abroad among the nations: But if ye turn unto me, and keep my commandments, and do them; though there were of you cast out unto the uttermost part of the heaven, yet will I gather them from thence, and will bring

21

them unto the place that I have chosen to set my name there. Now these are thy servants and thy people, whom thou hast redeemed by thy great power, and by thy strong hand. O Lord, I beseech thee, let now thine ear be attentive to the prayer of thy servant, and to the prayer of thy servants, who desire to fear thy name: and prosper, I pray thee, thy servant this day, and grant him mercy in the sight of this man. For I was the king's cupbearer. (Nehemiah 1:5-11)

Not only did he confess his sins, but he confessed those of all of Israel. The prophet recognized the need went far beyond himself. This situation impacted his friends, family and countrymen. This problem was bigger than just his state of mind just as our depression and anxiety are greater than ourselves. It impacts and influences everyone around us. It's not just about us. It's about our family and friends, our church and workplace. Something bigger than our happiness is at stake here. Let's step outside our bubble of selfishness and realize this journey will require us to think beyond ourselves and our desires, just as Nehemiah did. And while that sounds complicated, I promise you it is well worth it.

Now that we've established a firm foundation and cleared away the rubble, let's see if we have what it takes to accomplish the task ahead, or more accurately, if we're willing to do what it takes to achieve our goals.

RISE UP AND BUILD

SET YOUR MIND TO THE GOOD WORK

So built we the wall; and all the wall was joined together unto the half thereof: for the people had a mind to work. (Nehemiah 4:6)

After Nehemiah examined the foundation of the wall and deemed it sound, he explained to the people the plan to rebuild the wall. The inhabitants realized that this was a gargantuan task, but notice that at the end of verse 6, the Bible tells us they had a mind to work. What does that mean? It implies they were determined. The people purposed in their heart just as Daniel did when he refused to defile himself with the king's meat. They decided that they would do this, and nothing would stand in their way. They were resolute. Committed. Serious.

How about you? Are you committed to taking action? Most times, I think we're serious enough to complain about it but not

25

enough to take action. If we could have an instant fix, well, sign us up, but if we have to work for it, maybe not.

Are you ready for this? If we're not serious enough about the changes we wish to see to take action to achieve them, then we need to be quiet about it and let it go. No more whining and complaining! If it's important enough to complain about, then it's important enough to act on. So, if we're not willing to work, then we need to keep our mouths shut and accept things as they are. There are no instant fixes! Our problems didn't arrive instantaneously, and the solutions won't either. They require time and effort.

I'm ashamed to admit that, for many years, I fell into the category of caring enough to complain but no more. I wanted things to be different, but I wasn't willing to do what I knew to do to make them different. I had some warped notion that knowing what to do and doing it were the same thing, but that's not true. And knowing won't build walls or free us from our prison. The Bible spells this out in great clarity in James 1:22—*But be ye doers of the word, and not hearers only, deceiving your own selves.* We need to stop fooling ourselves and ask the tough question—how badly do we want to get better? Is it worth denying ourselves our creature comforts and favorite habits? Is it worth investing time and energy into it? Is it worth re-training our brain? How serious are we?

BUT I'M ALREADY SO TIRED

Some of you may be ready to throw this book across the room at this point, but I beg you, hang in there just a little longer. I know how you're feeling. Remember, I've traveled this same road, and I've been at this same point along the way. It goes something like this, "Yes, I'm serious about wanting to get better, but I'm already so busy and so tired. I don't know if I have the time and energy to put into it. It sounds like too much to handle right now." Am I right? (Maybe I should go into business as a mind-reader. I wonder how much money they make. LOL)

Honestly, I know where you're coming from, and I feel your pain, but this is what I finally realized. I can't afford NOT to take action. Getting rid of anxiety and depression became more than a hope or dream; it became a necessity. I finally realized I was dying a slow death, and enough was enough. So, I asked myself the following questions:

1) You say you don't have the energy to build these walls, but how much energy would you have if anxiety and depression weren't continually sapping it from you?

2) You say you don't have time to work on these issues, but how much more time would you have if you weren't crippled by anxiety and depression, which often results in long stretches of time where you're unmotivated to do anything?

3) You say you're busy, tired and weary, but what have you got to lose? If you build the walls and nothing happens, you won't be any worse off. On the other hand, if you build the walls and find that the added protection around your heart is hindering anxiety and depression from assaulting you, then you'll be much better off in the long run.

My point? You are already paying the price, so the question is, do you want to pay the price to be miserable or to be protected from that misery? The choice is yours, but once you make it, the real work begins. Remember, it's not enough to know; we must take action. We must have a mind to work.

You're Not Alone

Thankfully, this is not a one-man project. One of the major factors of anxiety and depression is loneliness. Whether we're sitting alone at home or in the midst of a congregation, depression can isolate us from our friends and family. Anxiety tells us that no one else could understand, so it's best to just keep our feelings to ourselves. Depression explains how no one cares what we're going through so we shouldn't trouble anyone else with our problems. Even in our stronger times when we feel the motivation to pull ourselves out of the pit once and for all, we have this insane belief that we got ourselves into this mess and it's our responsibility to get ourselves out.

Suppose Nehemiah had taken the same approach. After all, God told him to rebuild the wall. God burdened his heart about it. There is no record that God talked to anyone else about the situation or gave somebody else orders to rebuild the wall. The

RISE UP AND BUILD

task fell to Nehemiah, but fortunately, the prophet realized a powerful truth—God never intended for man to be alone.

From the beginning, in the Garden of Eden, God said, "It is not good for man to be alone," and He created Eve to be Adam's helpmeet. In the first book of the Bible, God established the importance of family and companionship. We need each other, and we ought to help one another as much as we can.

Two are better than one; because they have a good reward for their labour. For if they fall, the one will lift up his fellow: but woe to him that is alone when he falleth; for he hath not another to help him up. Again, if two lie together, then they have heat: but how can one be warm alone? And if one prevail against him, two shall withstand him; and a threefold cord is not quickly broken. (Ecclesiastes 4:9-12)

When I began my wall-building, I knew I wasn't strong enough to do it alone. After all, depression and anxiety are energy-sappers. I knew I needed help. So, the first thing I did was to ask God for help, and I have re-peated that prayer every single day of my journey, and let me tell you, friends, He has been faithful to provide strength despite things that have threatened to hinder my progress.

The next thing I did was to have a long talk with my husband. I explained to him about my journey and asked for his help and support. I even told him exactly what kind of help I needed from him. I needed him to be firm with me when I felt like giving up. I needed him to be the record keeper of how far I'd come when my brain refused to re-member. I needed him to encourage me and even to push me beyond my comfort zone. And above all, I pleaded with him to be pa-tient with me as I embarked on this arduous journey because I knew it wouldn't be easy. And you know what? Not only did he agree to all of these things, but he did even more. He decided to take the journey with me so that I didn't have to walk alone. Together, we've implemented these lessons into our lives and not only has it changed us individ-ually, but it has strengthened our marriage and our relationship with Christ.

I could have stopped there, but I didn't. I reached out to my family, my church, my friends and my readers. I asked for prayer and gave everyone permission to hold me accountable. If I wasn't sticking to the plan, I wanted them to let me know in case I was blind to it. (And if I was aware of it, I needed them to point it out so that I would at least feel guilty about it.)

I took my cue from Nehemiah 3 where the prophet gathered the people together and sorted them into groups, each responsible for a particular section of the wall. No one worked alone. No individual was isolated. They worked together, and collectively, they accomplished the task. If we want to build up our walls, we can't expect to do it alone, and we don't have to. Even if you don't have family or friends as supportive as mine, if you're saved, you have God, and really, He's all you need. So, don't use the lack of family and friends as an excuse. With God on your side, any task is possible.

SOME WILL TRY TO STOP YOU

Unfortunately, some will not make it easy for you, just as others didn't make it easy for Nehemiah and the Israelites. *But when Sanballat the Horonite, and Tobiah the servant, the Ammonite, and Geshem the Arabian, heard it, they laughed us to scorn, and despised us, and said, What is this thing that ye do? will ye rebel against the king? (Nehemiah 2:19)*

When some find out what you're up to, they will laugh at and criticize you. They will try to make you quit. Of course, the number one enemy here is Satan, but he may enlist the help of others in this fight. Those who will pull you astray. Those who will encourage you to give in to your old habits. Those who will not allow you to embrace the "YOU" that God wants you to be.

This is where that principle of having a mind to work comes into play. Not only do you have to purpose in your heart you will do what it takes to recover, but you will have to determine to do so despite what others think or say about you. Ignore those taunts that insinuate that you'll never be anything but what you are now. Don't listen to the pharmaceutical giants who try to convince you that your only hope for being "normal" can be found in the latest, greatest pill. Disregard those who dangle your past mistakes in your face. It may mean having to dissolve some friendships, but honestly, if that's how those "friends" act, you don't need them. They're toxic, and you need to let them go. Do your best to hang around with people who will encourage, inspire and support you. These are the ones who will help you build your walls.

AVOID DISTRACTIONS

That Sanballat and Geshem sent unto me, saying, Come, let us meet together in some one of the villages in the plain of Ono. But they thought to do me mischief. And I sent messengers unto them, saying, I am doing a great work, so that I cannot come down: why should the work cease, whilst I leave it, and come down to you? Yet they sent unto me four times after this sort; and I answered them after the same manner. (Nehemiah 6:2-4)

That's just like the enemy, isn't it? Just when you think you've got them figured out, they change tactics. When Sanballat and Geshem saw that their taunts and ridicule were not affecting the people, they tweaked their approach. If they could pull Nehemiah away from the job at hand, perhaps the people would grow weary and stop working. You know, take the cat away so the mice can play. Yes, the people had a mind to work, but how long would that last if their leader disappeared?

Fortunately, Nehemiah was too smart for their plan. He knew that they had no intentions of sitting down for a friendly cup of tea. He was acutely aware that they were out to destroy him and his efforts. So, he told them "no." Well, that didn't sit too well with these men—a lowly commoner disregarding them in such a way. So, they continued to "request" his presence.

Notice Nehemiah's response: *I am doing a great work, so that I cannot come down: why should the work cease, whilst I leave it, and come down to you?* I am doing a great work, and I can't stop right now. That is the attitude we need to adopt if we're going to rebuild the walls around our heart. No matter what comes our way—good or bad—we must avoid distractions! It is imperative that we awake every morning with the attitude that we are doing a great work, and we cannot and will not be stopped. We cannot afford to lose sight of our goal—to banish anxiety and depression from our lives once and for all. That task is great, so our determination will need to be great, as will our focus.

Sometimes the enemy's attacks come as full-on assaults, but often they take the form of distractions. The urgent comes into our lives, causing us to lose sight of the essential. Or even the good floats in, pulling our attention away from the best. Whether in the form of something good or bad, distraction will hinder our progress, and we must be on guard against it.

Nehemiah refused to be called away from his efforts. We must do the same.

WHEN YOUR EFFORTS FEEL INFERIOR

But it came to pass, that when Sanballat heard that we builded the wall, he was wroth, and took great indignation, and mocked the Jews. And he spake before his brethren and the army of Samaria, and said, What do these feeble Jews? will they fortify themselves? will they sacrifice? will they make an end in a day? will they revive the stones out of the heaps of the rubbish which are burned? Now Tobiah the Ammonite was by him, and he said, Even that which they build, if a fox go up, he shall even break down their stone wall. (Nehemiah 4:1-3)

Seriously? This guy won't quit, will he? The taunts didn't work. The distraction plan proved ineffective. So, he moved on to Plan C—make the hero feel inferior. Notice the words he used: *feeble* and *rubbish*. Not exactly encouraging, is it? And, not to be outdone, Tobiah adds, "Even if they did build the wall, it would be so weak and wobbly that a little fox could crawl on it and cause the whole thing to crumble." Deadly darts away!

The enemy will have you doubting yourself. Is it worth it? Are you doing it right? Shouldn't you be further along? He will make you feel inferior and try to convince you that your efforts are in vain. "After all," he will say, "you can build the walls, but as soon as something bad happens, they'll crumble again. Just wait and see." If we're not careful, we'll let him get to us, and we'll spend more time worrying than working.

Don't let the enemy tell you that you aren't good enough! Do not let him fool you into thinking that your efforts are worth nothing. Don't let him have the victory over you. It's not his. We are the victors. According to God's Word, we are more than conquerors (Romans 8:37), which means we can build these walls, and they will stand. Besides, we have the Master Builder on our side and if God be for us, who can be against us? (Romans 8:31)

We'll talk a little more about listening to the voice of the enemy in a later chapter, but for now, just remember that the enemy is a liar, and he'll say whatever it takes to get you to stop building. Don't give in to him and his wishes. Don't let him be your puppet-master by allowing him to control your actions by his taunts and scare tactics. He's just a bully trying to have his way, and you need to decide that you won't be bullied any longer. That's part of rising up. It's not just about building the walls, but it's about standing tall in the process, and it's impossible for someone who is being bullied to stand up tall. It's time to rise up. You are good enough because God said so. In fact, He thought you were worth dying for, so take that, enemy. God is doing a work in and through you, and He will complete it if you let Him.

Therefore, my beloved brethren, be ye stedfast, unmoveable, always abounding in the work of the Lord, forasmuch as ye know that your labour is not in vain in the Lord.
I Corinthians 15:58

RISE UP AND BUILD

STRENGTHEN YOURSELF
FOR THE TASK

Then I told them of the hand of my God
which was good upon me; as also the king's
words that he had spoken unto me. And
they said, Let us rise up and build. So they
strengthened their hands for this good work.
(Nehemiah 2:18)

I believe there's a lesson here for us. The first thing the people did after declaring they would rise up and build was to strengthen their hands for the work. Sadly, this step is often skipped because of one of two reasons: (1) People don't understand the significance of taking care of the physical in relation to dealing with emotional problems, or (2) People know but don't want to embark on that part of the journey.

Yes, I'm talking about diet and exercise. Do you realize that most of the diseases (physical, emotional and mental) we face today are linked to what we eat and our habits (or lack thereof) concerning exercise? It's true, and anxiety and depression are no exceptions. We are continuously feeding the very things that are draining our lives from us. And here's the crazy part, most of us refuse to change our eating and exercising. We refuse to strengthen our hands for the good work.

When I think about this, I'm reminded of the story of Naaman, the leper. Naaman was a mighty man and great ruler, but he was infected with the dreaded disease of leprosy from which there was no cure. By God's great grace, he learned of the prophet Elisha who could do miracles. When Naaman sought the prophet's help, Elisha sent his servant to tell Naaman that he should dip himself in the Jordan River seven times, and he would be healed. To say that the mighty man was upset would be an understatement. He was offended, first off, that Elisha didn't speak to him personally but sent a lowly servant. Second, the thought of sticking his big toe into the muddy waters of the Jordan was about as appealing as being buried neck-deep in sand, much less dunking his entire body in it seven times. Determined that he had wasted his time, he turned to storm off, but his servants stopped him and said, *My father, if the prophet had bid thee do some great thing, wouldest thou not have done it? how much rather then, when he saith to thee, Wash, and be clean? (II Kings 5:13)*

Naaman wanted drama. He expected that it would take so much more than a leisurely swim to solve his problem that he couldn't come to grips with the fact that his healing was much simpler than he imagined. He was willing to do something big but couldn't believe that this mere act of obedience would bring him healing. But it did.

Many people suffering from depression and anxiety are the same way. The problem is so big that they assume the solution must be too, but it's not, or at least, it doesn't have to be. We don't need magic potions or expensive treatments (though if you are currently using drugs to manage these issues, please do not quit at this point). I hope and pray that you'll find genuine healing with the elements that I will detail in this book and that, in time, you'll be able to stop taking medication. I'm not against medication, mind you, but the problem is that, like Naaman, we're seeking healing, and medication doesn't do that. It doesn't solve the problem; it only masks its symptoms, and many times, it doesn't even do a good job at that. So, while medication is sometimes necessary, our goal is to attain freedom from it as well as the depression and anxiety, and the first step is to address our physical health.

Remember, this isn't about a big drama. I'm not going to tell you that you have to live the rest of your life in a deprived state and never eat chocolate cake again. That's no way to live. We all need chocolate cake from time to time, right? I don't have the time or space in this book to address this issue in the depth that I want to, but I encourage you to pick up a copy of the companion book, ***Rise Up and Build Good Health***.

For now, let me say that I'm not talking about going on some fad diet or severe calorie restriction. Not only are those things unhealthy, but they are unrealistic because anyone who has tried them will tell you that it's nearly impossible to maintain that type of program long-term. And that's what we need

—a long-term solution. Remember, this isn't a quick fix. We're in this for the long haul, and that means making real changes that will last.

When it comes to physical health, you primarily need to pay attention to two things: (1) what goes in your mouth and (2) how much you move your body. So, let's break that down into small, manageable chunks.

DIET

What should go in your mouth? Let's make it very simple—if God made it, then let's eat it. If man made it, let's stay away. Empty your mind of everything you've been taught about carbs, fats, and calories and focus on the quality of the food. We all know that fruits and vegetables are superb for us and contain life-giving nutrients, so eat lots of them. You can change your entire way of eating by making little changes at a time. Trade out your soda for water. Try spreading avocado on your sandwich instead of mayonnaise. Make your meatloaf with oats instead of heavily processed breadcrumbs. Choose sunflower seeds instead of popcorn for your evening snack. Pretty soon those small changes turn into big results. And if you're serious, you can even find healthy recipes that will have you feeling better and more fulfilled than ever. (And yes, I share some of my favorites with you in ***Rise Up and Build Good Health***.)

What I'm saying is that you don't need specialized equipment or an expensive health program. There is no reason to weigh your food or count your calories. If you're eating the right kinds of food, everything else will fall into place. To get started, follow these simple steps:

1) Eat 4-6 small meals a day instead of 2-3 big ones. This is a huge component in healthy eating, especially on the emotional side of things. When we go long stretches without food, our blood sugar becomes unbalanced, which leads to mood swings and feelings of anxiety. Remember, though, the key here is that they must be small meals.

2) Use a small plate instead of a large one. If there's room on our plate, we will fill it to the max, so when we use a small plate, we automatically limit our caloric intake without having to do any counting or measuring.

A full plate tricks our brains into thinking that we're having more to eat, and our stomachs follow suit. Crazy, but it works!

3) Try to divide your plate into four sections. One-quarter is for your protein (typically meat). One-quarter is for your starch (rice, potatoes, bread, beans, etc.). One-quarter is for non-starchy vegetables (greens, asparagus, broccoli, etc.). And the final quarter is for fruit. If you eat in these proportions, you'll find yourself satisfied without being full, and you'll slowly see more and more energy in your life.

4) Drink half your body weight in ounces of water per day. In other words, if you weigh 150 pounds, half of 150 is 75, which means you need to drink 75 ounces of water every day. Water is the only real energy drink, and if we want to be energized, there is no easier way than drinking our fill each day.

That's it! See, no big drama, but I guarantee you that if you follow those four steps above, you'll notice a definite change in your well-being, including physical, mental and emotional.

Please keep in mind that you will probably feel worse before you feel better. When we deprive the body of the things it's used to getting, we experience a period called detox. What that means is that the body is ridding itself of the toxins that it has stored away in our fat stores. While safe and sound in our fat stores, they eat away at our health slowly, but once we force them out through changing our diet, those toxins are released into our bloodstream and digestive system, which means they wreak havoc on their way through. Imagine these individual toxins grabbing on to everything they can as the body works to sweep it through and out of our system. They don't want to go, and they'll fight to stay. Don't quit. Keep pushing them out by eating the right things. The detox can last anywhere from a couple of days to a couple of weeks, but afterward, you'll feel like a new person. It's an amazing transformation.

WHAT ABOUT EXERCISE?

I am not a gym rat. In fact, I don't like gyms at all (or rats, for that matter). If you do, that's great. That will make this step even easier for you, but if you're like me and dread the thought of exercise, never fear. There is hope.

I could go into a bunch of stats and research tests, but the entire purpose of this book is to simplify things, so let's boil it all down. The benefit of exercise is this: the more you move, the better you feel. The better you feel, the less anxiety and depression you experience. The less anxiety and depression you experience, the more you can enjoy life. See, I told you it was simple. God never intended for us to be sedentary beings, yet most of us live an inactive existence. We drive everywhere we go. We sit at a desk. We recline on the couch at night to watch television. We sit at the table to eat and in the chair to talk on the phone or browse the web on our laptop. In many ways, technology is a blessing, but when it comes to its impact on our health, it's not always in our favor.

What do we do about it? We don't have time to go to the gym. We don't have the money or space for expensive home equipment like treadmills or ellipticals. What are we supposed to do? First off, don't complicate it. Did you know that you burn more calories and use more muscles standing than you do sitting? It's true, so when possible, stand instead of sit. Next, find some activity that you like to do, and do it regularly. Maybe you enjoy playing sports or swimming or jogging. Do it! Try to move your body at least thirty minutes a day three to five times each week. You won't believe the difference it will make, and you'll soon discover that instead of costing you energy, it gives you a boost. And instead of eating away your time, it gives you more in return because you're more energized, focused and productive.

Personally, I have a serious issue with chronic dislocations of my joints, so most sports and weight training are not an option for me, though I do have to do some as part of the program to rebuild the strength in my joints and cure the instabilities. But I have found that I love walking and hiking. My husband and I take our dog out at least once a week and tackle a hike anywhere from four to nine miles. This is a wonderful time to spend with the family away from the hustle and bustle of life, and typically away from technology because there aren't even cell signals in most of the areas we hike.

For daily exercise, I go out each morning (weather permitting) on a prayer walk. Fortunately, I live within walking distance of a paved trail set up for walkers, joggers and bicyclists. I typically walk three to four miles, and it only takes me about an hour. I keep a brisk pace to keep my heart rate up but not so quick that I can't concentrate on my prayer at the same time. Let me tell you, there's nothing like a prayer walk to feel closer to God. I pour out my heart. He pours out His. It's a sweet and intimate time with just the two of us, and I wouldn't trade it for anything. So, you see, you can exercise your body and spirit at the same time.

Get moving and make it a habit. Not only will you strengthen your body, but you'll see amazing results in your mental and emotional factors as well.

Rest Is and Isn't a Four-letter Word

Lastly, when discussing how to take care of our physical bodies, we can't ignore the importance of rest. Yes, I know, you're busy. Yes, I know you have a lot to do and little time to do it. Yes, I understand that when you do take time out to rest, you feel lazy and have this weird assumption that everyone else is accusing you of being lazy as well. But rest is not an option; it's a necessity. Even God Himself set aside a time to rest. What makes us think we can float along on all cylinders and never take a break? It doesn't work. Our bodies demand rest, and if your body is anything like mine, it will stop and drop whether I want it to or not, so I've found it's better to stop and take a break before my body makes me stop.

Now, you may be wondering, how much rest do we need? Honestly, that all depends on the individual. If my husband sleeps six hours a night, he does great. As for me, my body needs around nine or ten hours. Yep, you read that right—nine or ten hours, and no, I'm not related to Rip Van Winkle. So, you know what I do? I sleep ten hours per night and get more done while I'm awake because I'm not spending all day yawning and trying to keep myself from dozing off. And if, by chance, I do still feel tired, I take a short rest around mid-day. I'm not much of a napper, so I seldom sleep during the day, but taking a few minutes to close my eyes and rest my body does wonders to refresh my mind and spirit.

Here's the key to finding out how much sleep you need: go to bed and wake up at the same time every day. My bedtime is 8:30, and I do my very best to be in bed by that time every night. The reason I do that is I'm most productive in the morning and least productive in the evening, so I have adjusted my bedtime to suit my schedule. By going to bed at the same time every night, my body automatically wakes itself up at the right time in the morning, typically around 6:30. I don't need to be jarred awake by an alarm clock. I don't have to get up before my body is fully rested. My body does the work, and I reap the benefits. You can do the same. Start by setting your alarm clock for the time you need to get up (until your body is trained to wake up on its own, you'll need to use the alarm clock). If you currently do not wake up before your alarm, try going to bed a half hour earlier each night for the next couple of weeks. If you're still not waking up before your alarm, go to bed a half hour earlier still. Keep pushing your bedtime back every couple of weeks until you consistently wake up before your alarm. This will give you a good indication of how much sleep your body needs. Once you've determined your body's rest requirements, try to meet that quota as much as you can. This makes a huge difference in energy levels and overall mood.

Okay, now that we've ensured our solid foundation and strengthened our hands for the work, let's take a look at what's involved in building up those walls to protect our hearts from the enemy's attacks and our own emotional currents.

SECTION TWO:

BUILD UP THE WALLS

AROUND YOUR HEART

RISE UP AND BUILD

THE WALL OF THE MIND

We've already seen that the Israelites, under the supervision of Nehemiah, had a mind to build the walls, but I feel it's important to note that they also had to mind their minds while they were working. Think about it for a moment. They were being ridiculed, threatened, laughed at, distracted and attacked. How easy would it have been for them to say, "You know what? We quit. It sounded like a good idea, but we've changed our minds. It's just too hard"? So, why didn't they? What kept them from throwing in the towel (or the trowel, in their case) and leaving Nehemiah to finish the work alone? It was the fact that their minds were focused on the task before them and nothing else. Or to put it another way, they were paying more attention to the battlefield of the mind than to the battlefield around them, and that's as it should be because the mind is indeed a battlefield, and it is here that many battles are lost. And let me tell you, no one is immune to these attacks.

THE POWER OF A SINGLE THOUGHT

In I Kings 19, we witness Elijah's flight from Jezebel and, consequently, his flight from the Lord's work. You see, God had placed him in Jezreel for a reason. God had a work for him to do, and He wasn't finished with Elijah. But in a moment of fear and desperation, Elijah listened to his feelings and the thoughts swimming around in his head that told him it just wasn't worth the fight, and he fled. At first, he went to Beersheba, about one hundred miles south of where he was supposed to be. Then, after the Lord's tender care of him there, he continued his journey south and ended up another two hundred miles away at Mount Horeb (also known as Mount Sinai). It was a holy place, perhaps the best place to get his act together. . .if God hadn't already told him to be somewhere else.

What truly amazes me is the encounter that takes place next. The Lord comes to Elijah and asks, "What are you doing here?"

Listen to Elijah's reply: *And he said, I have been very jealous for the Lord God of hosts: for the children of Israel have forsaken thy covenant, thrown down thine altars, and slain thy prophets with the sword; and I, even I only, am left; and they seek my life, to take it away. (I Kings 19:10)* There are many things wrong with Elijah's comments, but I don't have the time and space to go into that right now. Instead, I want to continue the story. Read on:

And he said, Go forth, and stand upon the mount before the Lord. And, behold, the Lord passed by, and a great and strong wind rent the mountains, and brake in pieces the rocks before the Lord; but the Lord was not in the wind: and after the wind an earthquake; but the Lord was not in the earthquake: And after the earthquake a fire; but the Lord was not in the fire: and after the fire a still small voice. And it was so, when Elijah heard it, that he wrapped his face in his mantle, and went out, and stood in the entering in of the cave. And, behold, there came a voice unto him, and said, What doest thou here, Elijah? (I Kings 19:11-13)

59

Again, there's so much that could be discussed here, but alas, I must press on to get to my point. After God had displayed His great power and manifest presence, he asked Elijah again, "What are you doing here?" Surely, Elijah was humbled by this event. The Bible says he wrapped his face in his mantle which is a sign of humility and respect. From that verse alone, it appears that God had gotten through to the prophet. We expect Elijah's next words to be those of sorrow and repentance. Perhaps a plea for forgiveness or a second chance. But no, take a look at what he said: *And he said, I have been very jealous for the Lord God of hosts: because the children of Israel have forsaken thy covenant, thrown down thine altars, and slain thy prophets with the sword; and I, even I only, am left; and they seek my life, to take it away. (I Kings 19:14)*

I assure you this is no typo, nor did I type in the wrong verse by mistake. Elijah's second answer was nearly identical to his first. He gave the Lord the same answer almost word for word. You know what that tells me? Elijah had been rehearsing. I believe that the forty-day trip from Beersheba to

Mount Horeb gave Elijah a lot of time alone with his thoughts, and it wasn't at all productive. It seems to me that Elijah rehearsed in his mind that same sob story so many times that he had it memorized and could probably spout it in his sleep. And that, my friends, is what happens when we allow our minds to dwell on the wrong things.

In her book, **The Best Yes**, Lysa Terkeurst put it this way: "We do what we do and feel how we feel because we think what we think." Oh, how true! Elijah was running from God because he felt like he was all alone in the battle and that God had let him down. From before the time he faced the 450 prophets of Baal, he was declaring that he was the only one left serving God. Evidently, that thought (false though it was) blossomed into fear, anxiety and eventually a rebellion so great that even the shaking of the mountain couldn't loosen Elijah's grip on his bitterness. He did what he did and felt what he felt because he allowed himself to think what he thought.

The mind is a battlefield, and every thought can be a dangerous enemy. Take care. Be "mindful" of what you allow yourself to dwell on. If you're not sure if the thought lurking about is friend or foe, run it through the filter of Philippians 4:8: *Finally, brethren, whatsoever things are true, whatsoever things are honest, whatsoever things are just, whatsoever things are pure, whatsoever things are lovely, whatsoever things are of good report; if there be any virtue, and if there be any praise, think on these things.* That will quickly help you to identify the thoughts that should be allowed to remain and those that need to be brought into the captivity of Christ (II Corinthians 10:5).

Never underestimate the power of a single thought!

DOES THE BIBLE TEACH POSITIVE THINKING?

The wealth and prosperity coaches of this world teach a principle called The Law of Attraction, also known as Positive Thinking. This philosophy is the belief that a person's positive or negative thoughts will bring about respectively positive or negative things. In other words, according to this warped teaching, we can control the outcome of our lives by thinking only the right things at the right times. The sad thing is that, like most lies, there is a grain of truth to this philosophy, though not in the way these coaches would like you to think.

Proverbs 23:7a says, *For as he thinketh in his heart, so is he.* Using that verse as their "proof text," these prosperity seekers claim that if you think you're rich, you'll become rich. If you think you're healthy, you'll become healthy. Like some magical field of dreams, if you think it, it will come. Sorry, but life doesn't work that way.

These teachings irritate me because they use the Bible as their proof, but what they're saying is distorting what the Lord is saying through His Word. If life were as simple as to think it and it will happen, then why do we need the Lord? Why is there heartache and disappointment? Why isn't everyone healthy and wealthy? Sadly, these prosperity seekers are leaving God completely out of the picture and saying that we are in control of our lives and futures, and it all boils down to merely thinking about what we want and believing it will come true. They have confused positive thinking with blind ambition, and they're leading people astray by the millions (and many of them are making millions of dollars in the process).

That being said, while we are not in control of our lives and futures, we are in control of our thoughts and emotions. We determine what we think about, and that's where the Biblical principle of positive thinking comes into play. Take, for example, Proverbs 23:7 again. *For as he thinketh in his heart, so is he.* Our thoughts cannot dictate our circumstances, but they certainly affect our emotions and even our actions. If we think angry thoughts, it's not long before we're upset and acting out in that anger. If we think negative thoughts, pretty soon we're depressed and snapping at everyone we come in contact with. Our emotions and actions follow our thoughts, so it's not rocket science to see that if we think positively (as Philippians 4:8 commands), we'll have more positive emotions and actions.

Romans 12:2 says, *And be not conformed to this world: but be ye transformed by the renewing of your mind, that ye may prove what is that good, and acceptable, and perfect, will of God.* We are not of the world; therefore, we shouldn't think as the world thinks. Instead, we are to be transformed by the renewing of our minds. To transform something means to make a drastic change. If your thoughts are anything like mine used to be, a transformation sounds like a good thing. I love the way the Merriam-Webster dictionary explains the word "renew." It means, "to make (something) new, fresh or strong again." New. Fresh. Strong. Talk about positive thinking! God is saying that if we want to change our lives drastically, we need to do some serious work on our thoughts. How? One step at a time. One thought at a time. Constantly on guard. Catching those treacherous trespassers and stopping them in their tracks.

Sounds pretty simple, but I assure you, it's hard work! Thoughts come and go by the hundreds, and to keep our emotions and actions in check, we need to closely monitor every idea that passes through our brain and run them through the filter of Philippians 4:8. If it's positive and uplifting, then it can remain. If not, give it over to God immediately. Keep in mind, I'm not talking about ignoring the thoughts and hoping they'll go

65

away. That does NOT work. Trust me; I've tried. I thought I was doing good by pushing them away, but the trouble was that I wasn't giving them to God. I was trying (in my own strength, I might add) to ignore them, but let me tell you, they're determined and adamant. More so than I am. We cannot simply bury them. We must turn them over to God and allow Him to do away with them.

Now, you may be wondering what exactly that means. How do we give our thoughts to God? The process takes a few steps, but they happen rather quickly and are quite effective. First off, accept responsibility for the thought. Remember, you have a choice about what you think. Second, stop that thought in its tracks and recognize it for what it is. If it's a realistic problem, identify it as such. If it's some fear-filled "what if," acknowledge that as well. You can't deal with an enemy until you've identified it.

Once you've acknowledged the thought and its value, give it to God verbally. If you have time, you can say a long prayer here, but if not, something short and sweet will do. For example, "Lord, this thought is weighing me down and causing me fear. I give it over to you and trust that You love me enough to work this situation out for my good and Your glory." From there, I've found it helpful to quote some Scripture or sing a gospel song. This keeps my mind occupied long enough for the anxious thoughts to slip away.

A good way to look at surrendering your thoughts to God is this example. The process of writing and publishing a book is complicated and involves many stages. Most of the elements I do myself, but to speed up the process with this book, I hired out some help. I turned the cover work over to one person, the description to another. Someone else was responsible for formatting, and another person did the logo. While each of them was doing his job, I was doing mine. Basically, I had turned over the responsibility of individual areas to them, and I trusted each of them to do their part. I didn't have to worry if it was getting done. I didn't keep checking in with each worker to make sure they weren't letting me down. Why? Because I knew each one and understood that I could count on them. By allowing them to do their part, I was able to focus on mine, and the entire process was smoother and much less stressful. The same holds true when we turn our problems over to God. We can trust Him to do His part because He's proven Himself faithful. And because He's dependable, we are free to do the work He has called us to do. We don't have to fret about whether or not God is capable of handling the task. He's got it! That is what it means to turn our thoughts and situations over to God. Give Him control and focus on the things He's given us to do that we can control.

Unfortunately, the battle doesn't end there because there are three other walls that need to be built to set up the perimeter around our heart, but I'll tell you the good news. Once you've built the first wall, the others go up much easier because they are each anchored to the previous one. For example, we've just covered the importance of filtering our thoughts, and that will help us with the next wall which is controlling what we say. Why? I'll let the Bible explain.

O generation of vipers, how can ye, being evil, speak good things? for out of the abundance of the heart the mouth speaketh. A good man out of the good treasure of the heart bringeth forth good things: and an evil man out of the evil treasure bringeth forth evil things. But I say unto you, That every idle word that men shall speak, they shall give account thereof in the day of judgment. For by thy words thou shalt be justified, and by thy words thou shalt be condemned. (Matthew 12:34-37)

What we think drastically affects what we say, and in the next chapter, we'll see that the words we speak hold the power of life and death.

THE WALL OF THE TONGUE

"You are such a loser."

"I am never going to lose this weight."

"I'll never feel better. I'm stuck in this endless sea of sickness."

"Why do I always do this? Why can't I do anything right?"

These were common statements from my everyday vocabulary. Comments of negativity and doom. Statements that left me feeling even more discouraged and deflated than I was to begin with, yet as hard as I tried to filter my words where others were concerned, I was downright careless with the proclamations I made to and about myself.

Maybe you can relate. You have a steady vocabulary of put-downs and condemnations. You call yourself names, perhaps even in a joking tone, but deep down, you know you mean every word. As you

71

head to the buffet for the third time in the past half hour, you label yourself "fatty." As you cry on your pillow at night, you berate yourself for being such a cry baby. When you fail to meet the deadline, the word "stupid" crosses your lips over and over again. Phrases such as "I can't" and "But I" roll off your tongue like a marble across glass.

It was only recently that I learned exactly how much damage I was doing to myself with my speech. In fact, it seemed that my own mouth caused most of my anxiety and depression. I was speaking myself into a tizzy, and I didn't even realize it until I came across this verse:

Death and life are in the power of the tongue: and they that love it shall eat the fruit thereof. (Proverbs 28:21)

Before we go any further, I want to read that verse again. *Death and life are in the power of the tongue: and they that love it shall eat the fruit thereof.* We have the power of life and death, and that power resides in the little member we call the tongue. The book of James has much to say about the tongue, and most of it is not good. It equates the tongue to a fire that cannot be tamed or quenched. So, if we can't quench it, how in the world are we supposed to build up a wall?

To begin with, we go back to the first wall and control what we're thinking. As we've already seen, the words we say come from our hearts and minds. We often use the phrase "think before you speak," but the fact is that we always think before we speak. We just don't usually think about the right things before we speak; therefore the wrong words come out of our mouths. We say things we don't want to say—things we know we shouldn't say. So, it goes without saying (no pun intended) that if we get our thinking under control, our speech will follow.

That's certainly the approach Nehemiah used. After all the opposition the people faced and the detrimental comments hurled their way, Nehemiah rallied the workers with his words. Check this out: *Then answered I them, and said unto them, The God of heaven, he will prosper us; therefore we his servants will arise and build: but ye have no portion, nor right, nor memorial, in Jerusalem. (Nehemiah 2:20)* When the en-

73

emy tried to tear down the people, Ne-hemiah sought to build them up with the power of words. God will prosper us. We are His servants. We will arise and build. Positive statements. Power statements. God-centered statements. These are known today as affirmations.

WHAT DO YOU SAY?

The word "affirmation" is another term that causes most hard-core Christians to balk. Isn't the practice of speaking affirmations a new age thing? Doesn't this go against the Bible? Actually, no. Speaking affirmations is another practice that has been adopted and transformed by health and wealth seekers. The issue is that these prosperity teachers instruct us to use affirmations to change our destinies, but instead of speaking truth, we are supposed to speak what we want to be true. The catchy phrase is "speak what you seek." So, if you want to be a millionaire, you should consistently use affirmations like, "I have more money than I know what to do with," "Everything I touch turns to gold," or "I will never want for anything in my life." The same principle applies to losing weight or getting healthy. Some traditional affirmations in this category are "I am in the best shape of my life," "I am healthy and trim," and "Food is no longer a temptation to me."

On the surface, this doesn't sound too bad, but as I said earlier, if you dig down, you'll see the root of the problem. For starters, none of those statements is true. Just because we want something to be true doesn't mean it is. I guess this is why these types of affirmations have never really enticed me because it doesn't matter how many times I say I'm healthy and wealthy, I know it isn't true. I only make myself a liar. Secondly, it's all focused on self and selfish desires. Where is God's will in all of this? It's all about me and what I want. And we know that's not what the Bible teaches.

So, with those accusations against affirmations, I considered them dangerous and tried to move on. But as the Lord worked on my heart, I realized that real affirmations are a good thing and can be used to help combat anxiety and depression, not to mention a host of other deadly darts from the devil.

Furthermore, he opened my eyes to many of the Bible "greats" who used affirmations—particularly David and Paul—to encourage themselves in the Lord.

What is a real affirmation? It is a statement or proclamation of something that is true, and in our situation, that comes directly from God's Word. Instead of proclaiming what we want, real affirmations state what God has said. And to use these affirmations as a weapon, I have found that it works best to make it personal. Don't just mindlessly quote a verse. Claim it! Put yourself into it, knowing that if God said it (and if it's in the Bible, He did), then it's true and can be believed. Over the course of a few days, I jotted down several pages of these, but I'll just share with you a few to give you an idea of how affirmations can be used to counter the attacks of Satan and our own fleshly nature (you know, like the negative statements we were spouting about ourselves at the beginning of the chapter), just like Jesus did during his forty days in the wilderness.

The Lord has planned my future, and I trust that it will all play out for my good and His glory. - Jeremiah 29:11

I declare myself to be free because Jesus Himself set me free. - John 8:36

I can do all things through Christ who strengthens me. - Philippians 4:13

I will not lack any good thing. - Psalm 34:8

My faith makes me whole in spirit, soul and body. - Mark 5:34

My body is a living and holy sacrifice unto the Lord. - Romans 12:1

I will be kind and do good to others. - I Thessalonians 5:15

I forgive those who hurt me because God forgives me. - Matthew 6:14-15

I honor God by taking care of my body which is His temple. - I Corinthians 6:19-20

There is nothing I will face today that God will not provide a way of escape. - I Corinthians 10:13

God is doing a good work in and through me. - Philippians 2:12-13

It may sound simple, but let me tell you, it is effective. Having these affirmations ready and speaking them when I feel the vicious attacks on my soul has kept me from sinking into despair when things don't work out the way I wish. I have found myself much more focused on God as my strength and refuge and less focused on my circumstances. These statements have helped me resist temptations and cravings and have even kept my attitude much more positive.

In short, affirmations do work, and there's nothing wrong with them as long as they are founded in and based on Scripture. I encourage you to give it a try. When the attacks come, instead of complaining or allowing yourself to be swayed by your circumstances or emotions, try speaking aloud some affirming statements from the Word of God. Make it personal. Apply it to your life right now. Claim God's promises. Hold fast to His truth. Something amazing happens when we turn our eyes off what we want and instead focus on the truth that God has given us. Try it and see, but remember, this is not a timid exercise. Speak it aloud and be bold about it. It will have little effect if you don't believe what you're saying. But if you do believe, let everyone know it, including the devil. Remember, he can't read your mind, so he won't know that you're quoting Scripture, but if you speak it, he'll know, and pretty soon, he'll flee. Put it to the test and be sure to let me know the results.

If you're not sure where to begin with Biblical affirmations, I encourage you to visit RiseUpandBuild.net. There you'll find free resources to aid in your battle against anxiety and depression, including a list of my own personal affirmations and an audio version you can listen to anywhere.

SOMETIMES LESS IS MORE

As I've already told you, I am writing this book from personal experience. I began this journey to freedom from anxiety and depression a couple of months ago when the Lord first spoke to my heart about writing this book. Since that time, I have spent many hours both learning and putting into practice what the Lord has been teaching me. Has it always been easy? Absolutely not. Have there been hiccups? Oh, yeah. But overall, I definitely see progress. And to be honest, some of the improvements I see are things I didn't even know to expect.

For example, here's something interesting I noticed this week. When something negative comes to my mind, I determine not to say it and cast the thought away as quickly as I can. The funny thing is I've discovered I have a lot less to say these days. Yes, my communication has decreased drastically, and after further study, I found out that's actually a good thing. Check out these verses:

Be not rash with thy mouth, and let not thine heart be hasty to utter any thing before God: for God is in heaven, and thou upon earth: therefore let thy words be few. (Ecclesiastes 5:2)

Wherefore, my beloved brethren, let every man be swift to hear, slow to speak, slow to wrath: (James 1:19)

In the multitude of words there wanteth not sin: but he that refraineth his lips is wise. (Proverbs 10:19)

He that hath knowledge spareth his words: and a man of understanding is of an excellent spirit. Even a fool, when he hold-

eth his peace, is counted wise: and he that shutteth his lips is esteemed a man of understanding. (Proverbs 17:27-28)

Whoso keepeth his mouth and his tongue keepeth his soul from troubles. (Proverbs 21:23)

He that keepeth his mouth keepeth his life: but he that openeth wide his lips shall have destruction. (Proverbs 13:3)

And there are many more verses in the Scriptures that discuss the importance of talking less. This is new territory for me. I don't like the quiet. When I'm with someone, I feel the urge to carry on a conversation (though usually, it's one-sided when speaking with my quiet-natured husband). When we're sitting in silence, it feels like there's something wrong. I get the impression that one or both of us is angry or upset, and I can't seem to resist the urge to fill the silence. But God has been working with and helping me to spend less time talking and more time simply basking in His goodness. It hasn't been easy, but it's been worth it.

By keeping the negative thoughts out of my mind and off my lips, I have not only affected my mood but also the mood of those around me. I have remained in a more positive frame of mind which has aided my focus, concentration and overall energy. I think we often fail to realize what a powerful impact our words have on our health and the health of those around us. I think back to the lyrics from the children's song, "Oh, be careful, little mouth, what you say!"

May our words be few today and only those that build up ourselves and others! If we want abundant life, we must rein in the tongue.

THE WALL OF THE EARS

If you're already working on the first two walls, you have a head start on this third wall: what you hear. It makes sense that we say what we think and hear what we say. The messages we take in each day affect our thinking, our mood and even our mental and physical health. Just ask Charlie Brown. Not once, but twice in the span of a thirty-minute Christmas special, the downcast character proclaimed something to the effect of "Everything I touch gets ruined." He thought it. He spoke it. He heard it. He believed it. And in his eyes, that statement came to life over and over again. God's word tells us, *Pleasant words are as an honeycomb, sweet to the soul, and health to the bones. (Proverbs 16:24).*

Sadly, our world is full of noise, and most of it is not positive. The people of Nehemiah's time could certainly relate. We know that they had taunts and insults hurled their way, and they had done well to resist the distraction. But the enemy does not give up without a fight, and sometimes he'll even enlist the help of those we thought were on our side.

And it came to pass, that when the Jews which dwelt by them came, they said unto us ten times, From all places whence ye shall return unto us they will be upon you. (Nehemiah 4:12)

Notice, it was their people who came to them, not once or twice but ten times, declaring that, no matter how fervently they worked, the enemy was going to catch up with them and destroy them. Some friends! They felt the need to spout this doomsday message over and over again, hoping to scare the people enough that they would cease their work. I imagine some of the workers began growing discouraged. I have no doubt that at least of few of them were wondering if all that work was in vain. Something about hearing that repetition of forthcoming gloom sent shivers up their spine and a sinking feeling in their hearts.

Thankfully, Nehemiah was wise enough to see what was going on and to lead the people in some hearing exercises. No, these weren't the type where the administrator of the test plays some sounds at varying levels, and the people lift a hand when they hear the noise. This was a hearing replacement exercise—one where the lies and taunts of the enemy were replaced with the truth of God's Word. *So then faith cometh by hearing, and hearing by the word of God. (Romans 10:17)*

In Nehemiah 8, we see the people meditating on the Scriptures and worshiping God. In the first part of verse 18, the Bible tells us, *Also day by day, from the first day unto the last day, he read in the book of the law of God.* Did you catch that? Day by day. Every day. Instead of allowing the voices of the enemy to be the only thing they heard, the people filled their ears, minds and hearts with the Word of God. They made sure they had something else to listen to besides the enemy, and we need to do the same.

LISTENING SUGGESTIONS

One of my favorite ways to accomplish this is by listening to gospel music, Bible teachings and sermons, and with today's technology, this is easier than ever. You can visit YouTube, iTunes, various podcasts and much more to find wholesome music and Bible studies to fill your mind with God's truths, and the best part is, most of it is free. This may not work for everyone, but I have found it easier to pay attention and keep my mind focused when someone else is speaking, and the beautiful thing about audio programs is that you can listen to them while you drive, do housework, exercise and much more. Listening–really listening–to things like this will help to keep your mind from wandering to negative things and dwelling on the what-ifs of life. It will also immerse your heart and mind in the truths of God's word, which is exactly what you need to combat the lies of the devil and the confusion that results from your discouragement and despair.

If you would like my help in choosing suitable material with which to fill your mind, feel free to contact me. I'd be happy to help. You can also visit RiseUpandBuild.net, where you'll find free resources, including playlists of Bible teaching, uplifting music, and clean comedy.

The key is to make sure you don't leave too much time for idle thoughts. This can lead to big trouble and deeper depression!

WHAT ABOUT MUSIC?

Martin Luther once said, "Next to the Word of God, the noble art of music is the greatest treasure in the world." I agree with him completely, but I believe that can only be true if the music we're listening to is the right kind of music. So, how does one define the "right kind" of music? Obviously, hymns are good, but what else? Southern Gospel? Contemporary? Classical? Country?

In years past, I set apart good music from the bad based on the lyrics of the song. If the words were genuine and uplifting, then I deemed the song right. If they weren't, then the song was off limits. This works in certain areas of music. For example, if a song promotes loose living, drugs, alcohol use or other immoral acts, it's quite obvious this is not something to which we should be listening. But with the more recent trends of Christian Rock and other hard-core music, where should we draw the line? Many of these songs have good, Bible-based lyrics, so does that mean they're acceptable?

A few years ago, I heard a message on this very topic, and I must admit that it's the best sermon on music choices that I've ever heard in my life. It was so direct and impactful that it has remained with me to this day, and the method outlined in the message enables me to determine whether a particular song or type of music is something to which I should be listening.

If you recall, the shepherd boy, David, played a vital role in the royal household before he was king. It was his job to play the harp for King Saul, who was often troubled by evil spirits. The Bible tells us that when David played, the evil spirits fled, and Saul was at peace. That's what music is supposed to do. It should bring about peace and cause the evil spirits to flee.

To determine if your music is good or bad, pay attention to how you feel while you're listening to it and immediately after. Are you in a good mood, or do you feel irritated and even angry? Do you feel at peace, or are your emotions in a whirlwind? Did the music leave you feeling refreshed or anxious? Then use these guidelines to weed out the music that leaves you feeling out of sorts. For me, I discovered that, even though Christian rock and Christian hip-hop songs often had quality lyrics, the nature of the music and singing style resulted in agitation and anxiety. So, I banned that music, along with other selections, from my music library. On the flip side, most Southern Gospel and some Contemporary Christian music made me feel uplifted and encouraged, which is what we should expect from music. I also enjoy select instrumental, classical and even soundtrack music. While there are no lyrics, the feel of the music itself will evoke certain reactions.

Listening to positive, uplifting music is a wise step in filling your mind with the truth of God's Word. After all, good music is nothing more than God's truth put to a melody.

Don't Believe Everything You Hear

I would like to have a word with the weatherman. He said that yesterday was supposed to be mostly sunny with a high of 72°—beautiful weather for taking the dog to

RISE UP AND BUILD

the lake. The only problem is that he was WRONG!

It was not mostly sunny; it was quite cloudy all day. It was also windy and cool. Thankfully, I had taken a jacket for the morning chill. I ended up wearing it the entire time. My hands were so chilled I could barely write. The temperature was 58° when I began my hike. It was 60° when I was done. Ooooh, heatwave!

I'm not complaining about the weather, mind you. The cool temperature was quite a relief from the extreme heat we've been dealing with. No, my complaint is not with the weather—it's with the weatherman. If he doesn't know what the weather will be like, he should just say so. It just goes to show us that we can't believe everything we hear.

We've already discussed how the world's teachings don't line up with God's Word, so we must be careful to block out their voices or at the very least, to take what they're saying with a grain of salt. Nehemiah learned that lesson as well.

Afterward I came unto the house of Shemaiah the son of Delaiah the son of Mehetabeel, who was shut up; and he said,

Let us meet together in the house of God, within the temple, and let us shut the doors of the temple: for they will come to slay thee; yea, in the night will they come to slay thee. And I said, Should such a man as I flee? and who is there, that, being as I am, would go into the temple to save his life? I will not go in. And, lo, I perceived that God had not sent him; but that he pronounced this prophecy against me: for Tobiah and Sanballat had hired him. Therefore was he hired, that I should be afraid, and do so, and sin, and that they might have matter for an evil report, that they might reproach me. (Nehemiah 6:10-14)

Shemaiah was supposed to be on Nehemiah's side. He was a fellow prophet and supposedly a good guy, but when he told Nehemiah that he should hide in the temple, Nehemiah knew that something wasn't right. Even though the source was trustworthy, Nehemiah was smart enough and clear-headed enough to run those instructions through the filter based on what God had already told him. When he did, he figured out that Shemaiah had been hired by Tobiah and Sanballat (yes, the same old enemy).

Their goal was to make Nehemiah fear for his life and run to the temple to escape his fate. But Nehemiah knew that his fate was in God's hands, and that Tobiah and Sanballat couldn't do anything to him unless God allowed it.

We cannot believe everything we hear from the enemy or even so-called friends. And we especially cannot trust what our emotions are saying to us. They are the biggest liars of all! They will tell us that we're all alone, that no one cares about us, that things will never get better, that we might as well help ourselves because no one else will do it, and on and on. Don't listen! Our feelings and emotions, when left to their own devices, will seek to do what Tobiah and Sanballat attempted to do to Nehemiah— they will make us fearful and ineffective. Don't listen. Do what Nehemiah did and compare the statements of your feelings to the truth of God's Word. Here's what you'll find:

Feelings say, "You are all alone." God says, "I will never leave you nor forsake you."

Feelings say, "No one cares about you." God says, "I loved you enough to send my Son to die for you."

Feelings say, "You're such a loser. You'll never accomplish anything." But God says, "You are more than conquerors through me, and you can do all things through me."

Feelings say, "You've tried before and failed. This time won't be any different." God says, "Though you fall, you will not be cast down, for I'm upholding you with my hand."

See what I mean? Don't listen to the myriad of voices around you. Tune in to the only one that matters!

RISE UP AND BUILD

THE WALL OF THE EYES

As I pulled into a parking space at the grocery store this morning, I immediately heard a deep, menacing bark. Being a dog-lover, I turned to see if I could spot the protective pooch, but what I saw was not the sight that I was expecting. In the van a couple of spaces down, a tiny runt of a dog stood on his hind legs in the passenger seat, his nose pressed to the window. I closed my eyes and shook my head, thinking that something had to be wrong with my eyes, but in that instant, I heard the bark again. My eyes snapped open, and I spied that same little runt of a dog.

By this time, my mind was swirling. I knew that there was no way that deep, ferocious bark could have been coming from that weeny of a dog. I mean, I've seen some big dogs with wimpy barks, but this just wasn't possible. As I contemplated what was going on, the barking started again, and sure enough, the little dog in the van was moving his mouth in a barking motion. Only it wasn't in sync with the actual sound of the barking. Confused to a new level, I looked around a bit more and suddenly understood what was going on. I had failed to see the giant German shepherd that was being walked along the grass strip of the parking lot. Evidently, the German shepherd had spied the little dog, too, and was wanting to get hold of it (tasty treat, maybe?). The little dog was merely barking in response to the bigger dog, but because the little dog was enclosed in the vehicle, his pitiful little bark couldn't be heard.

Finally, things made sense, and I could exit the car and go into the store, assured that I wasn't losing my mind. I did get a good laugh from the event. . . and a good lesson.

There are a lot of voices in this world. Voices that give direction. Voices that comfort and console. Voices that convict and voices that set at ease. And somewhere, in the midst of all that noise and all that confusion is the voice of Jesus. The voice that we should know and recognize. The voice that we should heed. But sometimes, I feel just like I did this morning. My ears are telling me one thing, but my eyes are telling me something else. My ears told me that the sound I heard was coming from a large dog. There was no doubt about it. . .until I spotted the little dog. Suddenly, I became less sure of what I knew to be true, and I was encompassed by doubt and confusion.

That's exactly where Satan wants us to be—paralyzed by uncertainty. You see, as I sat in my car this morning, despite being in a hurry to wrap up my errands for the day, I was mesmerized by the conflict between my ears and my eyes. And in that state, I couldn't do anything else. Everything else faded away as I focused on trying to figure out what was going on, striving to sort truth and error. All the while, my tasks were going undone, and that's right where Satan wants us. He desires for us to be confused, so dependent on what these little eyes see that we are willing to forsake the truth that we know deep down in our hearts. That's why the Bible teaches us to live by faith.

Sometimes what we hear the Lord saying won't mesh with what these human eyes see. God says, "I will supply all your needs," but your eyes are staring at this month's bank statement, and it's not pretty. God says, "This is for your good," but from where you're standing, the situation looks anything but good. God says, "I love you so much," but your earthly eyes see a circumstance that surely He wouldn't allow to happen to one He loves. Our ears hear His promises, but our eyes see evidence to the contrary. Which one is to be trusted?

Actually, neither. It wasn't my ear this morning that I needed to believe. It was God's truth. As I mentioned, I knew in my heart that the bark was from a large dog. I've been around enough dogs to know. That's why it's not enough to know or hear God's promises. We must believe them with all our heart. Then, when the eye is telling us one thing, we can check with our heart to determine the truth of the situation. If the evidence of the eye is contrary to the proof of the heart, well, then you have your answer.

I return to the old children's song, "Oh, be careful, little eyes, what you see." And while that is wonderful advice, I'd like to add to it, "Oh, be careful, little eyes, what you believe." It certainly would save us a lot of confusion!

WHAT ARE YOU LOOKING AT?

Did you know that our thoughts and actions have a tendency to follow our eyes? If you don't believe me, just ask a race car driver. I've witnessed many interviews with drivers where the person conducting the interview asks, "How do you keep from hitting the wall?" It's a valid question. I mean, those cars fly around that track at breakneck speeds, and often while packed tightly on top of one another. So, how do they keep from hitting the wall (and yes I realize that sometimes they don't)? But, in the interviews, every time the answer is the same —"I don't look at the wall."

Race car drivers know that their actions will follow their eyes, and whether they mean to or not, if they focus on the wall, that's where they'll end up. We see this same philosophy taught in the very first chapter of the Bible. Check out this passage:

And when the woman saw that the tree was good for food, and that it was pleasant to the eyes, and a tree to be desired to make one wise, she took of the fruit thereof, and did eat, and gave also unto her husband with her; and he did eat. (Genesis 3:6)

Did you catch that? The woman saw. The fruit was pleasant to the eyes. Yes, ladies and gentlemen, sin entered into this world because Eve was looking at something she had no business looking at. Of all the trees in the Garden of Eden, why were her eyes on this one? Why did she insist on gazing at the forbidden fruit? I don't know, but once she saw it, she couldn't resist. Unfortunately, I can relate.

Sodas and energy drinks are my kryptonite. I know they are horrible for me and contain nothing good whatsoever. I realize, despite what my feelings tell me, the drinks only harm me. I have repeatedly tried to give up these vices, but one thing gets me every time—I can't stop seeing them. They're everywhere. On billboards, in the grocery store, on the sides of delivery trucks, on the television. Everywhere I turn, there's a visual reminder of the tasty treat, and as soon as I see it, I feel like I have to have it. You know the old saying, "Out of sight, out of mind"? Well, the opposite works too.

By God's grace, I am breaking free from my addiction to sodas and energy drinks, and the only way that it's possible is by redirecting my gaze. I have set my mind to turn away from the things I shouldn't see and focus instead on something I should. Sound impossible? No. Difficult? Absolutely. But impossible? Not with God's help. To get started, let's discuss where NOT to look.

OUR WEAKNESSES

I don't know about you, but I am my own worst enemy. If there's a flaw in me, I'll find it. Whether it's physical, emotional, mental or even something in my personality or work ethic, I am determined to pick apart all my good characteristics to root out the one bad. Perhaps that's human nature. After all, the Bible is full of characters who focused only on their weaknesses.

When God called Jeremiah to prophesy to the people of Israel, the prophet argued that he wasn't the right person for the job because he was far too young. When the angel of the Lord appeared to Gideon, he called him a mighty man of valor even though Gideon was hiding from the enemy at that very moment. Still, the angel spilled out God's plan for Gideon to lead the people in an uprising, but Gideon commented that he couldn't possibly do such a thing because he was from an impoverished and lowly family. David was the runt of the household. And Moses? He had a laundry list of excuses why He wasn't the right man to lead the Israelites out of Egypt. In each case, the man saw only his weaknesses, but God saw what each one could be.

Yes, we all have weaknesses. We fall to temptation. We look at ourselves and find that we are lacking. Lacking skills. Lacking beauty. Lacking organization. Lacking self-control. How could God possibly use us because surely, with our many faults, we are unusable? Not true. Those are the lies of the enemy, and we must banish them from our minds, ears and mouths. Not only that, but we must learn to see ourselves as God sees us. Not what we are now but what we can become.

When the people of Nehemiah's time were rebuilding those walls, I'm sure they discovered some weaknesses. After all, had any of them ever built a stone wall before? Did they have the proper tools? The knowledge? The skill? If they had spent all their time examining their flaws, they would have never gotten the wall finished. Studying our weaknesses is a distraction and an impairment to running our race. And you know what else is a detriment? Looking back.

OUR PAST

The past is the past. It doesn't exist in this timeframe. We don't live there anymore. The only purpose the past should serve is what we learn from it. Take the knowledge; leave everything else. The guilt. The regret. The hard feelings. The rejection. Leave it all behind. We can't possibly conquer today if we're weighed down by yesterday. It's too much. The apostle Paul learned this: *Brethren, I count not myself to have apprehended: but this one thing I do, forgetting those things which are behind, and reaching forth unto those things which are before, I press toward the mark for the prize of the high calling of God in Christ Jesus. (Philippians 3:13-14)*

I love Paul's honesty here. He tells the church of Philippi, "Look, I haven't arrived yet, but I know one thing: I have to forget those things which are behind and press on toward the things to come." What excellent advice, except for one thing—how exactly do we forget the past?

Memory is a funny thing. I can remember lines from songs I learned as a child, anecdotes that I heard years ago, quotes from a television show and other non-important stuff, but I struggle to remember three of the four things on my grocery list and when my niece's birthday is. What's up with that? It often seems like the things we want to remember or even need to remember are those things that float away like a wisp of wind while the things we would give anything to forget appear to be permanently etched in our brains. I cannot explain how or why this happens except that I do know that memory is often linked to feelings and our various senses. The more intense the feeling and use of the five senses, the more likely we are to remember. It's kind of cool when you think about it, but how does that help us?

It doesn't really, but here's what does. Let's go back to our key verse for this study: *He that hath no rule over his own spirit is like a city that is broken down, and without walls. (Proverbs 25:28)* While we may not be able to consciously choose what things we remember and which ones we forget, we can make a choice whether or not to focus on them. We're talking about what we see, right? So, to "forget" the past, we need to turn away from it. Stop looking at it. Quit running it through the microscope, trying to figure out what you could have done differently. Stop the instant replay that circulates over and over again in your mind. Make a choice to put it out of sight.

I'd love to tell you that this is a one-time thing and that, once you set the past aside, it will remain forever hidden from view, but recall what I told you at the beginning of this book—this is not a quick-fix system. It will take time and consistent effort on our part if we want to put the past behind us, but I assure you, dear one, it is possible. And with our eyes facing forward, we'll be able to enjoy the view!

OUR FELLOW WORKERS

Another pitfall to avoid when it comes to our vision is looking around at what others are doing. In this day of social media, we are bombarded with images of model-trim bodies, gourmet meals that were "thrown together" after a long day at work, tidy homes, sizable bank accounts and so much more. Yes, after just a few minutes online, I feel like I could never stack up to everyone else. I don't have the perfect body. Unless spaghetti is considered a gourmet meal, I fail on that point as well. Tidy home? Not typically. Enormous bank account? Only in my dreams. It's downright depressing. Hmm, coincidence? I think not.

Looking around at what others have and we don't is a surefire way to create anxiety and depression in our lives. We feel deprived and left out, which leads to feelings of mistreatment (i.e. Why doesn't God bless me like that?) Pretty soon, these emotions escalate to bitterness, resentment and ingratitude. And the train doesn't stop there.

Let's go back to the wall at Jerusalem for a moment. What kind of chaos would have erupted if everyone was looking around at what somebody else was doing? I can hear the mutterings now. "How come I didn't get a hammer like that?" "Why is she working on the west wall while I'm stuck on the north wall?" "Whoa! He carried three bricks at a time. I wish I were strong like him." "If only. . ." Once again, this would have created havoc and major distraction. Everyone had a job to do, and it was essential that each person was focused on his/her job alone. There wasn't time to look around at everyone else. And I believe that's a big part of why they were able to finish the building of the walls in such a short amount of time.

You are you. I am me. You can't be me, and I can't be you. We each have our own strengths, talents and abilities, and God made us unique for a reason. He has a particular job for each of us to do, but we'll never accomplish it if our eyes are on everyone else instead of our own task.

I'm reminded of a conversation between Peter and Jesus after the resurrection. Jesus was giving Peter instructions on what He wanted the disciple to do next. And Peter, who had quite a knack for sticking his foot in his mouth, responded to the Lord's command like this: *Then Peter, turning about, seeth the disciple whom Jesus loved following; which also leaned on his breast at supper, and said, Lord, which is he that betrayeth thee? Peter seeing him saith to Jesus, Lord, and what shall this man do? (John 21:20-21)*

The Lord of the Universe had just given Peter a direct order, and all Peter could think to say was, "What about John? What's he going to do?" Jesus' answer is direct and quite comical. *Jesus saith unto him, If I will that he tarry till I come, what is that to thee? follow thou me. (John 21:22)* Let's boil that down—"Peter, it's none of your business. You have your orders."

God is telling us the same. We have our instructions. It doesn't matter what anyone else is or isn't doing. It doesn't matter if they're succeeding where we failed or failing where we succeeded. It's not our business! Our business is to follow God's plans for our lives.

That being said, while on this journey to overcome anxiety and depression, I discovered that not only did I need to watch out for comparing myself to others, but I also needed to make sure that I didn't compare myself to myself. Huh? I'll explain. Have you ever caught yourself making comments like "I used to be able to do this," or "When I was younger, I could. . ." When we do this, we're breaking two of our "eye rules." First, we're looking at the past. And second, we're comparing ourselves to someone else—a previous self.

You know what? I'm not twenty years old anymore, so it stands to reason that I can't do some of the things that I could when I was twenty. It doesn't do me any good to whine about it or to dwell on the "good ole' days. Press on. Move forward. I am a new me. You are a new you. Don't compare yourself to the you of ten years ago or even ten months ago. Each day is an opportunity to grow and improve, so each day, we'll be a different person than we were the day before. Remember, it's not about what we see. It's what God sees, and if we're living according to His will and doing all things for His glory, then what He sees is wonderful indeed!

WHERE SHOULD WE LOOK?

Now that we've established where we should not look, let's discuss where we should cast our eyes. For starters, it's obvious that we need to keep our eyes on Christ, for without Him, we can do nothing. We should look to Him and His ways, daily seeking His face and guidance. Beyond that, what are some other acceptable things our eyes can view?

What about looking to the needs of others? As we've already established, both anxiety and depression can lead to inward thoughts and a self-centered style of living. To feel better, we consume our time and energy on things for us, often failing to look beyond ourselves and see the needs of those around us.

As strange as it may seem, numerous studies have concluded that one of the best antidotes for anxiety and depression is reaching out to others. Simple acts of kindness like visiting a shut-in, baking cookies for a friend in need, or being a listening ear and a shoulder to cry on enable us to get our focus off of us for a while. In the process, we become more aware that we are not the only ones in need. And while I don't believe that misery necessarily loves company, I do know for a fact that it is comforting to know that we are not alone in the struggle.

The next time you're feeling down, decide to do something for someone else. It doesn't have to be a big thing or require a significant monetary sacrifice on your part. Just do something that will make someone else the object of your attention instead of yourself. Doing good unto others not only helps others; it also helps us.

SET A WATCH

I know I've said this multiple times already, but it bears repeating—treating anxiety and depression requires a lifetime commitment. While there will be progress and easier days, it is imperative that we not grow too comfortable and forget to set a watch around our hearts. No matter how much progress we make, the enemy will never stop trying to defeat us and to break down the walls that we have built up. We must remain ever on guard, ready for every attack, just as the Israelites did.

But it came to pass, that when Sanballat, and Tobiah, and the Arabians, and the Ammonites, and the Ashdodites, heard that the walls of Jerusalem were made up, and that the breaches began to be stopped, then they were very wroth, And conspired all of them together to come and to fight against Jerusalem, and to hinder it. Nevertheless we made our prayer unto our God, and set a watch against them day and night, because of them. (Nehemiah 4:7-9)

The enemy was angered and threatened by the people's progress, and they struck out. Because of the threat, Nehemiah set up guards to secure the perimeter day and night. The craftsmen worked with a tool in one hand and a sword in the other. Many of the men even slept in their clothing so that they could be ready to jump up and go to battle if necessary. They were on guard. They were prepared for any oncoming attacks. They were armed and ready, and we must be as well.

Throughout this book, we have covered the tools that you will need to find freedom from your anxiety and depression. These methods do work, and I am living proof, but you must remember that it is not multiple-choice. You must build and secure each wall for this to be effective. It will do you little good to watch what you see and hear while neglecting to control what you think and say. Two out of four walls will not keep the enemy out, and soon, even the two walls that you built will crumble. To protect the heart from the roller coaster of emotions that pull us this way and that, we must erect a secure perimeter and make the commitment to continue doing the things we know to do to keep our walls strong and defensible.

It is possible that, after some time, we may grow comfortable and a bit lazy in our efforts to protect our hearts, but I warn you, the results are devastating. Unfortunately, Nehemiah found that out firsthand. After the wall was built, a great revival took place among the people, and once things were settled, Nehemiah returned to his work elsewhere. Sadly, when he came back to Jerusalem, things were not at all as he had left them.

In chapter thirteen of the book of Nehemiah, the prophet visited Jerusalem and found the people living in sin and wickedness. They had forsaken the house of God and left it in disarray. They were working and selling on the Sabbath day, which was against their custom and God's law. They had married outside of their people, linking themselves with nations who served other gods. It was as if they had forgotten everything they had learned and for which they had worked so hard.

What happened? How did the people who were so devoted to serving God turn into such a wicked nation? In short, they grew lazy and stopped trying. With the walls of Jerusalem built and secure, they mistakenly assumed that their work was done, and they stopped putting forth the effort to serve God. They gave up control of their spirit, and they paid the price.

My dear friend, I know you're tired and weary. The journey has been long, and you've tried so hard to find joy and peace. I promise you, it can be yours, but it won't come without a price, and that price is time, energy and effort. But isn't it worth it? Yes, it's easier to fall into bad habits than it is to adopt new ones, but that's not to say it can't be done. As we've already determined, anything and everything is possible with God. He can deliver you from your anxiety and depression if you're willing to follow His Word and do the things He's asked you to do.

Are you ready for a change? Can you see yourself enjoying life rather than just enduring it? You now hold the key to your prison. You know what to do and even how to do it. The choice is yours. Shrug your shoulders and walk away, or rise up and build!

A FINAL WORD

It has been nearly four months since the Lord began dealing with me about this book and teaching me how to handle anxiety and depression Biblically. I wanted to write this final word to let you know that I am still succeeding in fighting off anxiety and depression. It has not been easy, and I have had my shares of ups and downs, but each day, I feel myself growing stronger. It is becoming easier to build up the walls of my mind, tongue, ears and eyes. I've become much more aware of what's going on around me and inside me, and the entire process has been liberating. I pray that you, too, will experience freedom through the principles laid out in this book and the other books in this series. May God bless you and deliver you from anxiety and depression.

My son, attend to my words; incline thine ear unto my sayings. Let them not depart from thine eyes; keep them in the midst of thine heart. For they are life unto those that find them, and health to all their flesh. Keep thy heart with all diligence; for out of it are the issues of life. Put away from thee a froward mouth, and perverse lips put far from thee. Let thine eyes look right on, and let thine eyelids look straight before thee. Ponder the path of thy feet, and let all thy ways be established. Turn not to the right hand nor to the left: remove thy foot from evil. (Proverbs 4:20-27)

RISE UP AND BUILD

RISE UP AND BUILD
RESOURCES

If you enjoyed this book and would like to find out more about dealing with anxiety and depression, I encourage you to pick up the two companion books: **Rise Up and Build Devotional** and **Rise Up and Build Good Health**. Each of these books build on the principles established in this book, giving you resources to heal your body, mind and spirit.

If you're looking for additional ways to combat anxiety and depression, I invite you to visit RiseUpandBuild.net, where you'll find numerous free resources to aid you in your battle toward freedom.

ABOUT THE AUTHOR

Dana Rongione is the author of several Christian books, including the highly-praised *Giggles and Grace* devotional series for women. A dedicated wife and doggie "mom," Dana lives in Greenville, SC, where she spends her days writing and reaching out to the hurting and discouraged. Connect with her on her website, DanaRongione.com, and be sure to sign up for her daily devotions.

Books by Dana Rongione

Devotional/Christian Living:

He's Still Working Miracles: Daring To Ask God for the Impossible

There's a Verse for That

'Paws'itively Divine: Devotions for Dog Lovers

The Deadly Darts of the Devil

What Happened To Prince Charming?: Ten Tips to Achieve a Happy Marriage Life and Live Happily Ever After

Rise Up and Build Devotional: 52 Inspirational Thoughts for Dealing with Anxiety and Depression

Giggles and Grace Series:

Random Ramblings of a Raving Redhead

Daily Discussions of a Doubting Disciple

Lilting Laments of a Looney Lass

Mindful Musings of a Moody Motivator

Other Titles for Adults:

Rise Up and Build: A Biblical Approach To Dealing With Anxiety and Depression

Rise Up and Build Good Health: Practical Insights to Heal Your Emotions by Healing Your Body

Creating a World of Your Own: Your Guide to Writing Fiction

The Delaware Detectives Middle-Grade Mystery Series:

Book #1 – The Delaware Detectives: A Middle-Grade Mystery

Book #2 – Through Many Dangers

Book #3 – My Fears Relieved

Book #4 – I Once Was Lost

Books for Young Children:

Through the Eyes of a Child

God Can Use My Differences

Audio Bible Studies:

Moodswing Mania – a Bible study through select Psalms (6 CD's)

The Names of God – a 6-CD Bible study exploring some of the most powerful names of God

Miracles of the Old Testament, Part 1 – a Bible study with a unique look at miracles in the Old Testament (4 CD's)

There's a Verse for That – Scripture with a soft music background, perfect for meditation or memorization

ACKNOWLEDGMENTS

This book would not have been possible without the help and support of the following people:

The Lord, my Strength and Song — Without Him, I can do nothing!

My husband, Jason

My loyal and high-ranking patrons:
    Lewis and Sharon White
    Patty Hicks
    Dawn Hodge
    Jo Anne Hall
    Peter Santaniello
    Lisa Gutschow
    Tara Looper
    Those who wish to remain anonymous

My church family who constantly asked, "When will the new book be ready?" They urged me to complete the task, no matter how overwhelming it seemed at times.

RISE UP AND BUILD

RISE UP AND BUILD